Poetry From Afar

MATTHEW

THANK YOU FOR JOINING ME ON THIS POETIC JOURNEY. I AM HONORED TO SHARE MY WORDS WITH YOU.

WITH GRATITUDE

J - A POET FROM AFAR
MARCH - 2025

Cover Design: Alta H. Haffner

SAKURA

Published by Sakura Book Publishing
sakurabookpublishing.com

FOREWORD

First, I want to thank Jim for the honor of writing the foreword to this wonderful book.

Poetry from afar is a collection of art and poetry giving us parts to the main theme, our poet's life. Each painting opens a memory or thought. Some lead to every star in the sky, and a few linger in most people's lives. This journey of ups and downs does have a beautiful ending, though. It introduces his thoughts on pain and leads to the gift everyone seeks. Love.

This book is a map of emotions. Each road leads to the center of his humble soul and the love of his beautiful wife. Sometimes, the only thing we can do in an unpredictable world is write about it and share. This is poetry from afar.

Charles R. Haffner – Poet & Author of My Dandelion Filled Heart; Living through Tears; Painting by Moonlight; Loving Alta in Haiku; If Love Was a Rose; Four Colors of My Life in Cinquain; Orchids Under the Stars: Seasonal Tanka Poetry; Yong in my Heart, and A Handful of Hearts

INTRODUCTION

Sometimes, I wonder why my prose comes out the way it does; it seems like I always start tryin' to write those rhyming words of poetry, only to end up with this same old unconstrained way of mine.

I have always been influenced by those masters of muses that intrigue my provocations, thinking this time, when I spill that ink, those scribbled words will not be just the same, only to drift back to this written delirium of mine.

After all, nothing is more elusive than a well-written poem's emotional charge. How we wonder, does word after word become so alive as to be felt deeply by the reader to never be forgotten?

After all, a poet is someone who burns with emotion, who—in the words of Mary Oliver—has "a mind that is lively and inquiring, compassionate, curious, angry, full of music, full of feeling" and who cannot bear to keep it in.

For you see, I will always be a poet with a unique style that reflects the genius that resides in my own thoughts, surrendering a glimpse of who resides within me.

It's simply the way it's meant to be, writin' these words of ordinary prose the way I do just for you.

I hope you enjoy this humble book of "Poetry From Afar"

GRATITUDE

"Dragonflies are the keepers of dreams… Dragonflies inspire… creativity."
— Agnes E.

` AMETHYST DRAGONS `

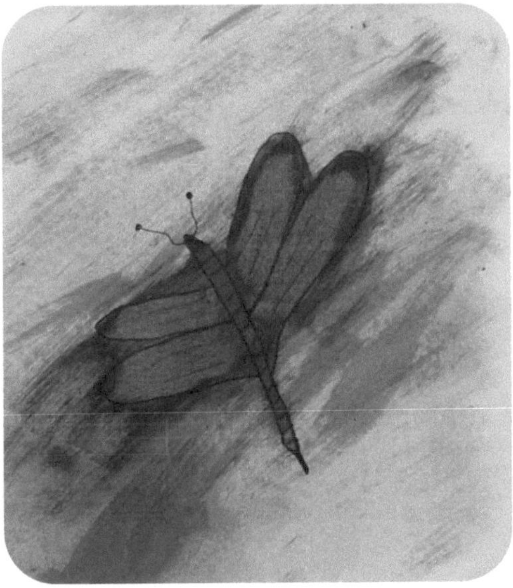

Artist Credits - © Alta H. Haffner
"Amethyst Dragon"

a *Haiku of Gratitude*

Summer's winged frailty
With the grace of an angel
Shades of purple hues

– Thoughts –
There are so many reasons to fall in love with dragonflies. They have intriguing stories to tell us. They make our world a more beautiful place to be.

GRATITUDE

With these words, I hope that you are curiously addicted to the simplicity of good poetry, art, and maybe even the pursuit of a beautiful amethyst dragonfly that might have the fragility and grace of an Angel.

This Haiku poem was inspired and written to give gratitude to the artist of the book cover, Alta H. Haffner. It is only fitting that it is the opening featured poem.

Alta has dedicated her life to the pursuit of helping others to achieve their literary and artistic dreams. Without her consoling way and wise mentorship, many poets, such as myself, would never have realized their dreams of publishing poetry for the world to witness.

This publisher and mentor of mine, she truly is a beautiful amethyst dragonfly with the grace of an angel.

Thank you dear friend for allowing me to realize these poetic dreams of mine.

RELECTIONS

"Some nights are made for torture, or reflection,
or the savoring of loneliness."

— Poppy Z.Brite

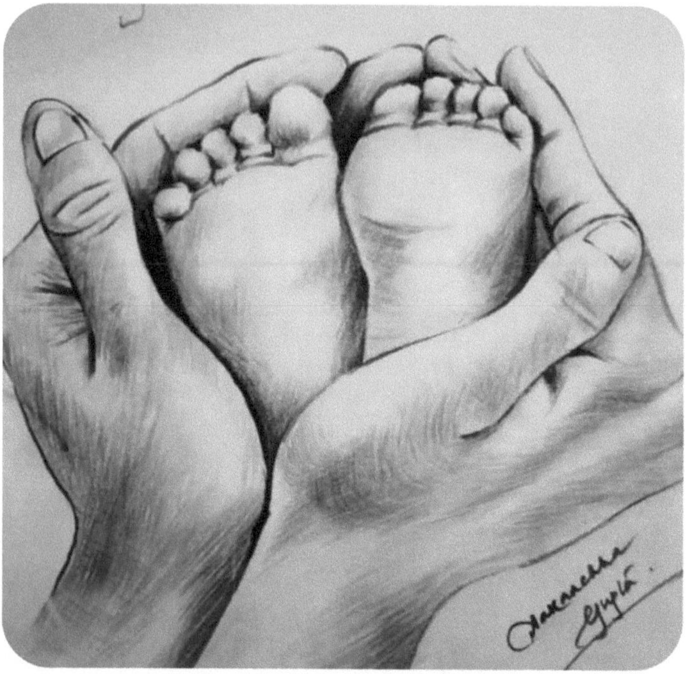

Artist Credits © Akanksha Gupta
आकांक्षा गुप्ता

"Once I could imagine my soul, I could imagine my death. When I imagined my death, my soul died. This I remember clearly. Why, I do not know. My body persisted. Not thrived but persisted."

- Louise Glück's "Echoes."

In Memory of Corporal Cody Gill Wade
a Fallen Warrior
Semper Fidelis

THAT MOTHER

That mother I know lost a child today; people came to grieve and console; she just sat and stared the day away you see she lost a child today —

Those people struggled to find the right words to say, trying anything to make that pain disappear, but all that mother could do was walk the floor in mistrust of her own reality. You see, she had just lost a child today, but in truth, that mother lost her child last month —

Most of the people who came with nothing to say just went away with nothing to say; some said they would call, and still, some just stayed with nothing else to say; those people who came to grieve with that mother who lost a child today, but in truth, she lost her child last month, but really she lost that child last year —

Now all those people who came to grieve with nothing to say are all away; that mother sits alone and struggles all day bearing witness to a pain kept buried deep inside her soul, for you see that mother lost a child today, but in truth that mother she lost her child last month, but really she lost that child last year, and again on each day after, even today —

– Writer's Thoughts –

I wrote this with grief in my soul for a friend and a mother who lost a son to a War's post-traumatic experiences, because you see that mother she lost a child today, but in truth, she lost her child last month, but in reality, she lost that child last year and will lose that child again with the passing of each day to that damn War's PTSD.

Rest in Peace Brother
Until we meet in Valhalla

Artist Credits © Eva Cruz

“You were born "you", but through self-cultivation and letting go of old patterns, you will quietly blossom into your "true self". Tea leaves live and witness this on a daily basis.”

— Paul Quintero
Zen Monk/Instructor
ordained by T. Deshimaru. Dharma art

MOMENT OF AWARENESS

Tell your story
Exclaim it, compose it
Shout it if you have to
But just tell it

Many won't appreciate it
Some will thoroughly renounce it
But most will thank you for it

By exclaiming your story
By confiding your words
By letting others know
A feeling of relating will evolve
A sense of commonality
A sense of understanding

It's that moment of awareness
Of never feeling alone again
So just tell your story
Exclaim it, compose it
Shout it if you have to
But just tell it

– Writer's Thoughts –

I write because it brings me so much peace and for me it is a sacred healing act of reclaiming my right to be here, my right to express myself and to experience the fullness of my being.

Artist Credits © Skandi Dawani
" Eye in the Sky "

"To fall in love with someone's thoughts - the most intimate, splendid romance."

— Sanober Khan

DARK LOVE AFFAIR

It's been a passion for awhile for many years now, actually,
one that keeps me gratified with titillating tryst

Always there, never asking much of me
just there like an intriguing utopia
with a diligent provocation filling that everyday calendar

Passing the precious time with complexities that fuel desires
for harmony

Tantalizing with an air of stupefying complacency
luring my idioms into corridors of creativeness

This relationship that bewilders
that connection that leaves me yearning further
that love I have for those words
my dark love affair with poetry

Jus' so you know, it's been a passion for a while that darkened
affair with this poetry

– Writer's Thoughts –

I do not write about things as if I have invented them.
I write about those things that inspire.
And because writing gives birth to a calm inside me
where there was once darkness.

Artist Credits © Skandi Dawani

"I think you get meaning through repetition."

— Damien Hirst

ALWAYS THE SAME

My mind tells me to write more poetry, telling me it won't be the same; but those doubts linger, those thoughts of provocation shredded into triviality of endless burdens by my own expectations

Somehow consuming my precious time preparing for that next literary pursuit, thinking this time the outcome might be different

Wanting to be wrong, but it's always the same, don't know exactly why, don't know how exactly; it just happens, always to be the same

Like the repetition of my intentions, it's always the same

It's just always the same

– Writer's Thoughts –

Repeated forms and regular arrangements have been used in art since ancient times. The simple act of repeating the same unit over and over again creates new narratives and interpretations. Artists seek variety but always find repetition. Always different but always the same

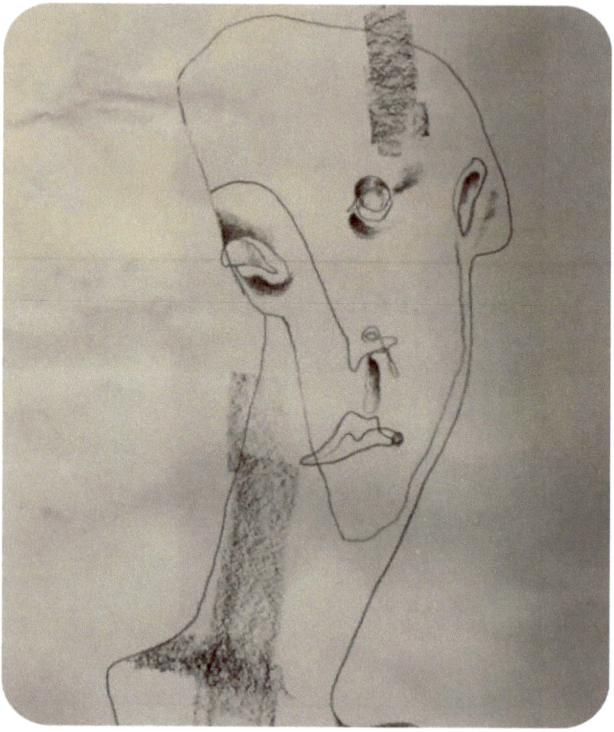

Artist Credits © Emma Eevantytär

"Poetry is a mirror which makes beautiful that which is distorted"

- Percy Bysshe Shelley

DISTORTED REFLECTIONS

Poetry takes me to a place of who I once was, a place of
reconsideration, a place of divergence from those reflections

Through these written introspections, those distortions from
another time, another place, offer a focused clarity, a place of
possible meaning, a place of echoed meditation

Compiling these words the way I do is like peering into an old
broken mirror, just seeing images of an aging face I want to
forget, a place far from that distorted reflection

These words just represent a place of departure from a shapeless
narrative that once was; It's just a distorted place that writes this
poetry the way it does

– Writer's Thoughts –

Thinking back on how I evolved as a poet, the one constant that remains is my distorted views of a past life that still visits me from time to time. I know not everyone is in harmony with their memories. Some choose to ignore them, while some ignore them because of the discomfort. For me it's probably both. It simply must be that distorted reflection writing these words of poetry the way I do.

Artist Credits - ©Kinga E. Vnuk
" Into the Light "

"I shouldn't precisely have chosen madness if there had been any choice, but once such a thing has taken hold of you, you can't very well get out of it."

- Vincent van Gogh
The Garden of Saint Paul Hospital, 1889.

INWARD

Sometimes I have this sense of just drifting along with the tides of life not able to recognize the shores of my own reality

Wandering, only to find myself with a compelling desire to liberate an inner self, searching for a quiet truth, one that will guide me along a path toward a greater awareness

Desperately wanting to ignite that light inside, illuminating that dark corridor complicating those thoughts of mine

Understanding that it's only then the clarity of my visions will become pronounced as I look inward to an awakened spirit thriving within my heart and soul

Looking inward, it's only then I can see that dark madness that had taken hold was a choice of my own making

It's only then I can travel along a path toward a greater awareness;
It's only then —

– Writer's Thoughts –

I once read that our visions only become clear when you can look into your own hearts. Those who look outside, are dreamers; those who look inside, are awakened.

Artist Credits - ©Vicki Sullivan

"Again and again, the cicada's untiring cry pierced the sultry summer air like a needle at work on thick cotton cloth."

– Yukio Mishima, Runaway Horses
(The Sea of Fertility, #2)

FURIES OF MY RECITATIONS

Been thinkin' lately about that fury in which I recite that poetry of mine with, its methodical repetition and all, been recollecting that I unfailingly repeat it aloud from memory until those words harmonize into a lyrical lullaby —

Some might suggest that these verses dripping from a newly acquired ink quill are simply verbiages of a late-night insomniac, maybe so —

Some might say that these furies of my recitations that I scroll represent a genius that resides in my own thoughts, maybe so —

What I say is, these recitations of my fury, with their methodical repetition and all, are just dark riddles seanced from an unwelcomed late-night delirium —

So, in summation, those words that I harmonize into a lyrical lullaby consoling your impressions with furies of my recitations the way I do —

It's just what I do —

– Writer's Thoughts –

Just thoughts on this fury of my recitations that I write for you the way I do; you know it's just what I do.

Artist Credits © Skandi Dawani
"Staring"

"You are who you are until you aren't anymore."

- Caitlín R. Kiernan
Agents of Dreamland
(Tinfoil Dossier, #1)

IT'S JUS' ME

Sometimes, I can't understand who I am, staring into my soul is like looking into a dark abyss, jus' seeing someone that you think I am

It's a feeling of desperation that haunts my thoughts, tryin' to be that person you hoped I'd be, but in reality I'm jus' staring into a reflection of who I wanna be

Peering into my own introspections, witnessing a portrayal through a lens of unpleasant scrutiny, always with the same mirrored reflection, jus' tryin' to be who I wanna be, not the one you think I should be

For you see, I'm jus' out here being who I wanna be, as you you stare inside of me, thinkin' I'm somebody you want me to be

Cause it's jus' me being who I wanna be

It's jus' me —

– Writer's Thoughts –

I feel I'm always staring into my soul seeing a reflection of who I want to be, but, still struggle after all these years not to be someone that the tribe wants me to.

I once read a quote that rings so true for most of us "Love what your heart sees, and be what you want to be."
It's as simple as that — jus' be who you wanna be!!

Artist Credits - ©Vicki Sullivan

"All are lunatics, but he who can analyze his delusion is called a philosopher."

- Ambrose Bierce
"The Collected Writings Of Ambrose Bierce"

MY POETIC ABSURDITY

I know, I have this raw way about me, it's that unconventional style that coerces these words of poetry the way it does

Sometimes, I think it's just the simplicity of my deliberations dictating those idiocies of my mind's curiosities

I know, that mere words can never really capture those soulful fragments hidden deep within the complex recesses of my mind, but I still write them anyhow

Sometimes, it's just that lure of life's lunacy urging me to shape a delusional expression of sorts

I know, it's just me over-scrutinizing things, prompting that eccentric style of mine exploiting this poetry the way I do

Sometimes, I know it's simply the life in my head spewing these absurdities the way I do

It's just what I do —

– Writer's Thoughts –

I know that I should seize this world of mine as it really is, rather than to empower my own delusional absurdities. But, it's much more satisfying letting that madness caress that eccentric style of mine exploiting this poetry the way it does.

Artist Credits © Pita Nketiah
" Light and Shadow"

"Submission does not mean being weak or passive. It leads to neither fatalism nor capitulation. Just the opposite. True power resides in submission---a power that comes from within. Those who submit to the divine essence of life will live in unperturbed tranquility and peace even when the whole wide world goes through turbulence after turbulence."

- Elif Shafak
The Forty Rules of Love

SUBMISSION

Been pondering a lot lately about submission, believing I've solved the mystery; seems so complex at times, but yet at other times can be quite uncomplicated, tho'

Been supposing that submitting to a quietude, opening up, and just letting it go, or maybe even letting things penetrate, enduring them, bearing witness to them, just seems to be the way to go

Been convinced submitting to those fears, anxieties, and pain might serve a purpose after all, might even be useful for the soul to let those things take a natural course, it's rather quite uncomplicated you know

Been supposing that sometimes we should just let that scar tissue form on those tender wounds, or maybe even from time to time let those scars reopen, turning that despair into a contrivance capable of forward progress

Just been thinking a lot lately that surrendering to it, accepting it, is quite uncomplicated, as you know submission just maybe might be the way to go after all

- Writer's Thoughts -

The reason why many are still troubled, still seeking, and still making little forward progress is that they haven't yet come to the end of themselves yet.

Artist Credits © Sara Fatah Samsom

"I felt so isolated, so broken, so lonely. I felt like no one on earth could understand me. I didn't even give them the chance. I just assumed they would never understand and used that assumption to block them out all the more."

— Michael J Heil

BEEN THINKIN'

In those moments of loneliness that plague my thoughts, I have learned how to make time pass, but what I recollect is that I can never stop thinkin' about you

It's those feverish ways that occupy my considerations, those obsessions with preludes of yearnings, craving for the touch of your divine tenderness

It's those pains of separation, those feelings of divergence, with a void in my spirit that pines for a distant warmth that only you can tend

It's in that sleepless solitude those words of longing never seem to fall short of articulating feelings of loneliness dictating my thoughts

Cause it's all I do, just thinkin' about you when that love thing touches my mind —

– Writer's Thoughts –

I read somewhere that overthinking during separation and the eventual loneliness accompanying it is like thinking yourself out of happiness. Which, by the way, I have done many times before. But in reflection, I have never once managed to think myself into happiness, especially when that love thing touches my mind.

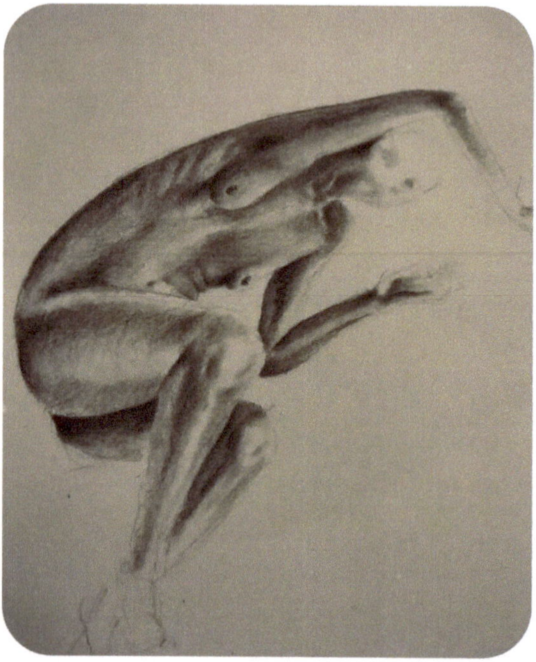

Artist Credits © Emma Eevantytär

"I have absolutely no pleasure in the stimulants in which I sometimes so madly indulge. It has not been in the pursuit of pleasure that I have periled life and reputation and reason. It has been the desperate attempt to escape from torturing memories, from a sense of insupportable loneliness and a dread of some strange impending doom."

- Edgar Allan Poe

LONELINESS

That darkness of winter carries with it a sense of shaded loneliness that seems to breathe with an aura of isolation

It's that aloneness that taunts the dark seclusion tormenting my soul; it's that solitude I crave, assembling those demons that once were part of me

It breathes that fear, with murky despair seeping into a fragile sanity that only I can restrain; it's that reality of isolation that torts this tired old my spirit of mine

It's that darkness of winter carrying a sense of shaded loneliness, breathing fear into a into a fragility that covets the solitude tormenting my soul

– Writer's Thoughts –

In those times of solitude,
we can often feel a sense of aloneness, an isolation that
breathes fear into a into our vulnerabilities.
But, the irony of it all is it's the time you most need to be by
yourself. In many ways It's one of life's cruelest insults.

Artist Credits © Eva Cruz

"We lead a Zen life to actualize our karma.
It's not about being holy. It's just about freeing ourselves from the weight of our past and directing our minds to what exists in front of us."

— Paul Quintero
Zen Monk/Instructor
ordained by T. Deshimaru. Dharma art

HARMONY

On those days that I allow my thoughts to yield to a peaceful way, there is always a sense of delicate peace that caresses my spirit

On those days, it's with this poetry I find myself lost in the depths of a poetic communion, an accord of sorts with the demons that once tormented a soul

On those days, I find the strength to liberate those vulnerabilities that have troubled me; it's through these words of poetic unity I've discovered the melody of harmonious balance

It's only then I'm truly at peace; it's only then

– Writer's Thoughts –

"The mind has a powerful way of attracting things that are in harmony with it, good and bad." — Idowu Koyenikan (2016)

It's with these words I find a constant reminder of my frailty and the struggle to achieve a harmonious balance.

Artist Credits © Kinga E. Vnuk
"Lavender Dream Reprised"
Oil on Canvas

"Out beyond ideas of wrongdoing and right doing there is a field. I'll meet you there. When the soul lies down in that grass the world is too full to talk about."

- Rumi

INTO THE SILENCE

When the soul struggles to be at peace, the world around has become too uproarious with fever

It's then I need to be alone; it's then I need to amuse this unrest in seclusion

It's then, in that solitude of stillness, that I can imagine a path into a place of peaceful calm, a place of truce, a place of waveless tides of tranquility

Into that silence, I'm free of unrest to ponder without conversations, without the annoyance of fellowship, with only the connection of my soul in that sequestered serenity

It's only then I can find a path into that silence, a place I need to be, a place of peaceful truce

– Writer's Thoughts –

There are times we all just need to be alone with our own thoughts of ponderance when the world around us becomes too loud with uproarious distraction. It's then we need to be alone the most with a quietude, a place into silence.

Artist Credits © Kinga E. Vnuk
" New Hope"
Oil on Canvas

"We have seasons when we flourish and seasons when the leaves fall from us, revealing our bare bones. Given time, they grow again."

— Katherine May
Wintering: The Power of Rest and Retreat in Difficult Times

HOPE

Winter carries with it a sense of shaded loneliness, breathing with an atmosphere of opaque solitude

It's during times of the dark, shortened twilight that those echoed reflections seem to possess a deeper intention about them

It's in those moments of review that life seems to meander, embracing the stillness with thoughts of a gentle solace residing inside our souls; it's in that solitude we can allow ourselves to slip into moments of intuition with reflections of restorative insights

It's through those long, dark winter introspections we can begin to understand the fragmented narratives of our lives without the distractions of the chaos around us

It's only then we can begin to flourish with hope, revealing a different kind of consciousness that meanders inside our souls

– Writer's Thoughts –

Wintering can be a dormant period in life when you're cut off from the world, feeling isolated in solitude, cast into the role of outsider with our own thoughts. As a poet, I flourish in it; I can spend hours in silent pursuit to understand the fragmented narrative of life . There is nowhere else to be, after all, in this time of wintered reflections, it can be a time of self healing, a time of a different kind of consciousness, a time of hope.

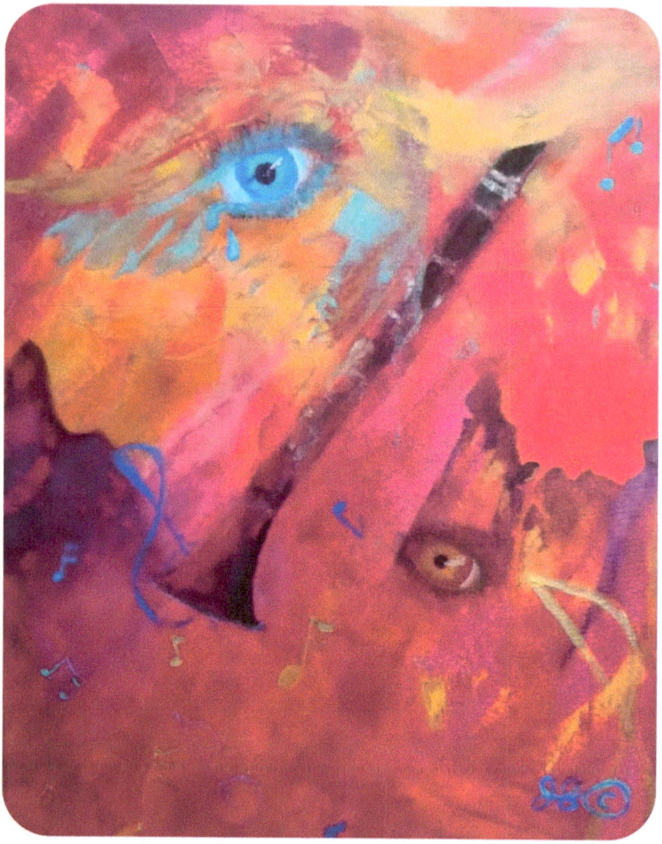

Artist Credits © Jenny Lou Crate Pena

"It is the nature of the earth to shift. It is the nature of fragile things to break. It is the nature of fire to burn."

- Susan Meissner
The Nature

FRAGILITY

Just another love thing that I can't ignore anymore, the same old tired story of a spirit flaming out through misguided representations

In my defense, it was with stupidity that I got too close to those matters of infatuation, eventually turning into lairs of those false desires

I clung to every word as if they were the gospel, not being able to quit, like an addiction I couldn't get enough, seems like I was just fine being used to kindle someone else's selfish attitude, being that flame of personal necessities and all

As I knew it would, that fire consumed my fragility, at the end of my wits, with no excuses, no trepidations as those instruments of necessity extinguished the passions of my soul

Like a box of matches, all used up with no more strike left; just sitting here with the ashes of my demise, writing this poetry just one more time about this love thing that I can't ignore anymore

– Writer's Thoughts –

Perhaps the most difficult poetry to write is that which explores what the conscious mind is tempted to ignore, which can only reveal itself in the unfettered flowing of poetry.

Artist Credits © Eva Cruz

" The universe wants you to be where you are. You have been invited to participate in it freely. "

— Paul Quintero
Zen Monk/Instructor
ordained by T. Deshimaru. Dharma art

INNER VOICE

It's that voice inside reciting those words written with a rhythmic tone articulating each inscription as they are conceived, overseeing the perception, reassuring that the foolery will be deciphered and accurately detailed along the way

That inner voice we visualize as we compose, expressing creative thoughts into harmonious representations

That inner voice soothing the soul, easing us into a writer's calm, lifting those words from our recollections, affirming our poetic undertakings are suitable for consumption

Revealing those sober thoughts lying deep interred inside of me, giving those words sensibility

That guiding inner literary voice of mine, reassuring that the foolery will be deciphered and accurately detailed along the way

– Writer's Thoughts –

Our writer's inner voice helps us build ideas that come through our minds. You think about a word, and then your inner voice and brain collaborate pleasantly and engagingly.

Your inner writing voice creates your brand. You get to know a writer because that inner voice has drawn your attention.

Let your words reveal your voice, your mind, and your ideas. It's all about making something creative from your words, even if they are sometimes just accidental

Artist Credits © Skandi Dawani

"This is my sin for giving in to my own weaknesses. My heart just couldn't keep up with the gigantic gap between dreams and reality."

— Fernandes

PENALTY OF SIN

When all said and done
Explaining a life of awful caricature
Wishing to be lifeless
Lifetime of living in a brine of guilt
It's the penalty of sin
Afflicted by corruptions
Anguish of an irreparable life
Chained to denial with no immunity
Like soulless pages of a dark book
Residing in the lyrical songs sin
Composing that final musical note
Suffering punishment for a lifetime of living in
that brine of guilt
It's the penalty of sin

– Writer's Thoughts –

Remorse emerges not in the absence of guilt but in our efforts to flee it. In the end, it is not your sins you hate but yourself and the efforts to escape it.

Artist Credits © Skandi Dawani

"Amy [Winehouse] changed pop music forever, I remember knowing there was hope, and feeling not alone because of her. She lived jazz, she lived the blues."

— Lady Gaga

THE BLUES ARE STILL BLUES

You tell me my poetry makes you blue
If I wrote you a gentle poem, could it bring you quietude
Would you take this gift - I wrote for you
Would you say this poem sings the blues
Would you say this is just another poem
Would you give this poem back to me
Saying this poem doesn't bring you quietude
Would you confess this poem is not a gift at all
Would you say this is just another poem that makes you blue
If I wrote this poem for you
Would you take my gift - that made you blue
Or would you say the blues are still the blues

– Writer's Thoughts –

Seeing this enchanting painting for the first time, even before I knew the title ` The Blues Are Still the Blues `. I felt it. The sadness that comes from life that we simply just don't sign up for. I thought maybe writing a gentle poem could it bring some quietude to it.

Wondering if I wrote this poem, would it be a gift, or would it just be another poem about the blues If I wrote this poem.

MATES OF THE SOUL

"As a young man, I wrote many love letters during my \`Travels\` to a special one that was afar. What I have come to understand is that every letter of love lies naked in one's soul; each word is only a mirror of the heart revealed undisguised to that one adored the most.

Through my years, I've come to appreciate that some letters of love may take the whole of our lifetime to write."

— a Poet from afar

Artist Credits - ©Airesh Kate Caliso

" You are the unwritten poem that I always carry
folded in the pocket of my heart."

- Curtis Tyrone Jones

POETRY FROM AFAR

I have seen a thousand sunsets, a thousand sunrises, I have seen a thousand moons waiting to glow brilliantly in the velvet black hiding just beyond the twilight

I have seen the oceans as smooth as painted blue silk, transparent as glass, moving with a majestic calm

I have known peaceful earthy silence; I have known the heartless silence of the darkness; I have known silence when everything is enchanted and stilled by the eye of the sun; I have known the sweet serenade of love filled with passion; I also have felt the silence when that eloquent poetry ceases to amuse the one I adore.

But—
All this I did without you.
I would gladly have forgone all this for the sake of one day being with you, hearing your voice, gazing into your calming eyes, and above all, feeling your beautiful soul.

My love, from afar, as I write these words, I want to remind you that when two souls are one, they hear each other, even in silence.

When my thoughts flow from pen to paper, I want you to feel my words of tenderness above that silence, to remind you that you are truly special to me, that you have consoled my soul in your calming way.

With each word, I want to remind you that I love you as no one ever will.

- Writer's Thoughts -

` Poetry from Afar ` was inspired by the sense that every beat of my heart is a love letter that needs to be penned. In truth, perhaps this poetry from afar is simply for the pleasure of everyone, and or anyone who just needs to read those love things that I so take so much pleasure in writing.

Artist Credits - ©Jenny Lou Crate Pena

"Owning our story can be hard but not nearly as difficult as spending our lives running from it. Embracing our vulnerabilities is risky but not nearly as dangerous as giving up on love and belonging and joy—the experiences that make us the most vulnerable. Only when we are brave enough to explore the darkness will we discover the infinite power of our light?"

— Brene Brown

SHE

It was the way she saw me when I showed her my vulnerabilities
It was her forgiving way of pretending that I had none to reveal
It was the way she uncovered that fragility, eliciting a spirit only she could have understood was deep inside of me

It was the way she cared for my decaying soul as we explored the darkness together, conquering those anxieties that she pretended were not alive inside of me

She had a way of telling my story that once was imbued with an eternity of darkness, now ushering in a sunshine guiding me to a better way
It was just her way of pretending that I had no vulnerabilities to reveal that saved me

It was just her way

– Writer's Thoughts –

The world to me has always had its way of balancing things. My life has not always been great. But with the support and console of that special 'She' in my life things always turned out ok. Even though things may seem dark there is always that bright spot, for me it is just her way that saved me.

Artist Credits © Skandi Dawani

"The distance between two minds is understanding, between two hearts is trust, and between two souls is love.
Trust is like love. It can't be seen, but its value is immeasurable."

- Frank Sonnenberg
Listen to Your Conscience: That's Why You Have One

TRUST

Just can't explain it, like that thing awakening in my soul when I catch the scent of the rain or when I see the sun and moon rise, with all those setting colors, a fire looms inside, luring my undivided intentions

It's almost like that time I let my heart fall for those things that enlivened this deprived spirit of mine; it was only then I could allow those complex but simplistic vulnerabilities to be exposed; it was only then I could open that weakened soul one more time, allowing that spirit of trust to enter, just one more time I kept telling myself

You know what I mean, giving a witness to those vulnerable parts of ourselves to someone else, allowing them entry into our complex vulnerabilities

Trusting those secrets into the open hands of others, letting them peer into that deprived spirit of mine, trusting them with the truth living within my soul

Allowing that spirit of trust to enter just one more time

I kept telling myself, just one more time

– Writer's Thoughts –

When I was thinking about allowing the mate to my soul inside this complexity of mine. I had to remind myself to have enough courage to trust love one more time , just one more time.

Artist Credits © Rebecca Ray H Waldman

"I do not write about love as if I have invented it.
I write about love because thoughts of you
inspire self-forgetfulness.
And because writing about you gives birth to a star.
These stars sit inside me where there was once
darkness."

— Kamand Kojouri

MUSE TO A POETIC SOUL

A soul falling so ever deeply in adore… the type of fall that only a poet's words can speak

A muse from a brief encounter that returns to dreams, never to be forgotten with a sense of poetic consummation

A provocateur inspiring awe and apprehensions of love with just a hint of lust in everyone with eyes to witness
A consuming constitution evoking the minds of artists, poets, and troubadours alike with temptations of creativity

A shimmering reflection of a soul evoking a sense of yearning desire to be worthy of this luminous being of our allure

This unnatural, dream-like muse to a poetic adore, the type of provocateur that only a poet's words can write about with such provocation

– Writer's Thoughts –

The poet, songwriter, or artist has a unique relationship with the muse. Painters are inspired by their models, poets dedicate their finest work to their muse, and troubadours express their yearning for the Beloved in song.
You have a poet's soul if you fall deeply in love… so deep that you must find new ways to express it.

Artist Credits © Pita Nketiah

"Why Do I Write? Isn't it obvious?
I write because these words form a bridge
that takes me to you.
Go to my desk and ask for my pen.
Swift through the once naked pages and ask the ink."

- Kamand Kojouri

IT'S JUST MY WAY

I always look forward to the day that I compose this poetry just for you, it's the day I allow my heart to surrender to its weakest desires

It's the day that I allow myself to feel alive again, the day that my spirit is free, it's the day that I allow my soul to experience passion once again

It's simply the day that I adore the most, it's the day when I write these words of poetry to the one who has caressed my soul in a such gentle caring way

I know you wonder why I am this way, what these words are meant to be, or what inspires me to write this love poetry that I compose just for you, It's just my way

It's simply just my hopeless romantic way

– Writer's Thoughts –

As writers we are always looking for inspiration for our next write, when I saw this drawing I was reminded that I've always been a hopeless romantic when it comes to those love things, it's just my way.

Artist Credits © Skandi Dawani

"The more I reach for her soul, the more I connect with mine."
- Merlin Franco
Saint Richard Parker

THAT SOUL

There's this soul I've fallen for; it's a consoling type of spirit that only comes along once in a tendered life

It's the type of soul that each time you feel its presence, thoughts are gathered with hypnotizing desires for your consideration

It's the type of soul that you might ponder even when you shouldn't be, a type you long for, a soul that gives life to an old, weakened heart, one that demands warmth from those darkest recesses of a forbidden passion

It's just that kind of soul I always somehow fall for; you know, that soothing type of spirit that only comes along once in a tendered life

– Writer's Thoughts –

Kindness and caring are ambrosia for the soul. I've always found that a glimmer of hope in your heart is better than darkness in your soul.

Artist Credits © Skandi Dawani

"Someone I loved once gave me a box full of darkness. It took me years to understand that this, too, was a gift."
- Mary Oliver

IT'S BEEN A MINUTE

It's been a minute since I thought about those love things; I know it's a lot like riding a coaster of emotions

I know, at times, it's a lot like navigating a black hole with no compass into an abyss of darkened, skewed complexities

I know the truths of those overwhelming depths that we plunge to explore our heart's desires, to understand, to harness those things we feel towards others

I know my spirit endeavors to mimic those yearnings for a mate of the soul, the one that I have searched the world over, only to find that darkened abyss of skewed complexities once again

I'm sorry, but it's just been a minute since I thought about those love things

It's just been a minute –

– Writer's Thoughts –

Sometimes, if we are fortunate enough in those darkest moments, we discover the greatest gift of all; we learn that pursuing our heart's desire to find the mate to our soul doesn't always end with that love being reciprocal. It's been a minute, but I have realized sometimes, we don't have to waste a lifetime to harness that gift of wisdom those skewed complexities of love can nourish.

Artist Credits © Skandi Dawani

"Every portrait that is painted with feeling is a portrait of the artist, not of the sitter. The sitter is merely the accident, the occasion. It is not he who is revealed by the painter; it is rather the painter who, on the colored canvas, reveals himself."

— Oscar Wilde

PORTRAITS OF A SOUL

When a poet cannot stop themselves, it's then they are in the right place; it's then that they are consumed by passion, that artfulness of the pen, composing with a fervor behind their words, and it's then that poetry becomes a portrait of their soul

This is the way I feel when my thoughts caress these words that I harbor inside; it's with each written expression that my soul can speak what has been inside since the first time I witnessed her exquisite way

It's only through these proclamations of poetry that I can truly capture the emotions that console my spirit when it reflects on what her presence means to me

It's those thoughts of her providing a warm consolation as I allow my soul to surrender to those provocations and compose these words to the one who is adored by me the most

It's only then that a portrait of the soul be revealed by the emotions harbored from within

It's only then –

– Writer's Thoughts –

I once read that if you paint a portrait of love in your heart and you will feel loved. Often when I'm inspired to write I find those words being harbored inside my soul much as a portrait of my provocations.

Artist Credits © Skandi Dawani

"I desire to be with you. I miss you. I feel lonely when I can't see you. I am obsessed with you, fascinated by you, infatuated with you. I hunger for your taste, your smell, the feel of your soul touching mine."

— Jack Llawayllynn

HER ADDICTIVE PERFECTION

Was it wrong that her perfection was everything he desired, was it wrong to lust after her calm, alluring way, or her sharp sense of spirit that somehow plagued his soul at first glimpse

Was it wrong to adore those seductive sounds consummated with her soothing, graceful voice, with an intellect more endless than the utopias

Was it wrong to steal a glimpse of what she held sacred deep inside, her secrets, her desires, her passions, her hopes, and dreams; I ask you, was it wrong to yearn for her euphoric, additive way

Was it wrong to covet the way she carried herself in such an elegant way, to believe how fortunate he was to have found this spirit that graced his presence in such a perfect way

I ask you was it wrong to desire her in such a euphoric, additive way

– Writer's Thoughts –

I've always desired to be with this mate to my soul. I miss her when she is not near. I need to feel of her spirit touching mine. I think it's her perfection that consoles this soul of mine, always wondering is it wrong to desire her in such an addictive way?

Artist Credits © Pita Nketiah

“For you and me, the highest moment, the keenest joy, is not when our minds dominate but when we lose our minds, and you and I both lose it in the same way, through love."

- Anais Nin
Fire: From A Journal of Love - The Unexpurgated Diary of Anaïs Nin (1934-1937)

LOVING HER MADLY

I want to stroll hand in hand, bathing in your vulnerabilities, claiming your sorrows, sharing your oddities, not expiring until the twilight has been fulfilled

I want to be at your side as you consummate your deepest suspicions, as your heartaches bleed and finally sever from your agonies

I want to be that final glimmer of hope inciting every complexity of your confessed kept secrets

I want to smile as you smile
to laugh as you laugh
to cry when you cry
to feel our soul's touch

I want to be your confidant to roam hand in hand until the darkness has been devoured

I want to be those embers kindling the heap of ashes smoldering our lusts, renouncing our minds into a fiery longing

I want to lose my mind with you, to stroll hand in hand, bathing in your vulnerabilities until our soul's touch

– Writer's Thoughts –

I once read a quote by Anais Nin that lingered with me today; it's about the moment we realized that having those longings for love often causes us to lose our minds. It's even sweeter when those losing minds are consummated with the one who is driving you crazy with fiery lust in the first place.

Artist Credits © Skandi Dawani

"My heart made it's choice, and it chose you."

— Colleen Hoover
Maybe Someday

I CAN ONLY IMAGINE

I can only imagine our first kiss
Our first time together
The first time our eyes meet
The first time we embrace

I can only imagine our first romantic, intimate experience
I can only imagine what it would be like if we connected; you and me
Would we be devoted to each other
Would we be amazing together
Would it be extraordinaire

I can only imagine what we would share
What would it be
I can only imagine

– Writer's Thoughts –

I wrote this poem to imagine the way my heart would race
When a special someone was close, I would see her face from a distance.

When our eyes would meet, my heart would skip a few beats.
I could only imagine the way she would take my breath away when I finally realized she was not just a dream.

Artist Credits - ©Erin Murphy
"Spiced Butterscotch"

"It's painful, loving someone from afar. Watching them – from the outside. The once familiar elements of their life reduced to nothing more than occasional mentions in conversations and faces changing in photographs….. They exist to you now as nothing more than living proof that something can still hurt you … with no contact at all."

— Ranata Suzuki

WITHOUT YOU

There's a darkness that follows, a past that torments, threatening to complicate

Our hearts beating as one, breathing from the same rhythm, needing to have you near

It's when I'm with you that the sadness wilts, feeling alive again, caressing your passion, tasting your aroma

With a craving for the next moment I am with you, because afar, I'm lost without you

– Writer's Thoughts –

I read a quote once by Ranata Suzuki that just felt right for this piece "If you cannot hold me in your arms, then hold my memory in high regard.

And if I cannot be in your life, then at least let me live in your heart." Because afar, I'm lost without you.

Artist Credits © Alta. H. Haffner

"The moon will guide you through the night with her brightness, but she will always dwell in the darkness, in order to be seen."

— Shannon L. Alder

ITS JUST HER WAY

I knew it was just her way, she had that contemplating way about her, I could see it in her eyes as she gazed with peaceful serenity into that Moonlite evening, it was as if she yearned for a gentle rendezvous with that one adored the most, for you see it was just her way

You just knew her tender but spirited way could some how coexist with her courageous soul, with the aura of an angel, but a fierceness of a fighter; it was just her way

This angel that I know, composes poetry with the winds of the immortals but with a gentle touch of an eminent laureate

She moves through this world with a peaceful solace, but at the same time belongs profoundly to this earth

For you see that angel of mine, it's just her way — It's just her way to be

- Writer's Thoughts -

I was inspired to write this piece to the gentle serenity of this art. My mind's eye immediately cast an impression of one of "Poetic Reflections". As I composed the words, along the way I was drawn back to the artist who I have considered a poetic angel that watches over this tortured soul of mine.

Artist Credits - ©Erin Murphy

"You may be sensitive inside, but what I see on the outside is a soldier."

- Lauren Graham
"Someday, Someday, Maybe"

LETTERS TO MADEMOISELLE

My Dear Mademoiselle,

My heart will always follow yours; this letter is written in the ink of passion with thoughts of you; it's a story of love that will endure, a journey of two connected souls, a tale of love that will never wither, a bond that will never release

I'll paint the pages with the ink that drips from my heart, every word a promise, every line a vow; these words I pen for you will follow your heart wherever it goes, to love you forever, from then until now

Our love will be a masterpiece,
a work of art that will never cease, a love that's written in the stars, guided by the ink of my heart's memoirs

So let my heart follow yours, written with this ink from a devotion, in this journey of two connected souls, a tale of love that will never wither, a bond that will never release, that love I carry for you

Regards,
Your Soldier Afar

– Writer's Thoughts –

Soldiers have always written letters to those special someones, and I was no exception. I have composed countless letters to those loved far away during my years of military service worldwide. These words of poetry represent a time in life that I now refer to as `Letters.` A time in a young soldier's heart that once was.

Artist Credits - ©Vicki Sullivan

"Love is hard to find, hard to keep, and hard to forget."
— Alysha Speer

YESTERYEAR

The past beats inside me like a pulsation of the heart, like a piece of art capturing those moments that are gone forever, feeling like a parody impossible to impersonate

Memories of yesteryear, where my thoughts meander, always finding a way back to her

Just a portrait painted in a mind forever returning to a love not forgotten, a dear departed only to leave those distant memories, the ones that can't be stolen from deep within my soul, those impressions brushed with colors of the darkest hues in that void of my broken core

An image from a heart's desire that once tasted so sweet but is now served with a dash of pain sprinkled on a wounded spirit

These lonely memories of yesteryear serve as portraits of a love that once was

– Writer's Thoughts –

The worst part of holding onto memories is not the pain.
It's the loneliness of it.

Artist Credits - ©Kimberly Brake

"Having so thoroughly reinvented herself, she had little sense of belonging anywhere and was, at heart, very solitary."

— Rhonda K. Garelick,
Mademoiselle: Coco Chanel and the Pulse of History

DARK PROVOCATION

In this old poet's eyes, she had a look of temptation about her
that offered darkness to my soul

She had a mysterious seduction with a wickedly salacious gaze,
I could barely breathe as she decoyed me to explore the depths
of her dark abyss, devouring my soul with her provoking way

Without discretion, her touch was like a sinful euphoria to my
addiction that I craved with the lure of her poetic enchantment

This mystifying Muse of mine with her dark provocation, like
an addiction that has devoured my soul, it's the lure of her way
that brings me back time and time again to compose these
thoughts of literary passion for this mysterious Mademoiselle
that has become the center of my poetic euphoria with her
dark provocation

– Writer's Thoughts –

Each day, I seek inspiration to compose these thoughts of poetry that burden me. Searching endless galleries of Art in hopes to feed that dark-provoking addiction to find the perfect muse. Only to reach the same conclusion every day that it's those love things inspiring these thoughts of my pen. Always to return to the lure of my desires for this mysterious Mademoiselle that has become the center of a poetic euphoria with her provocative way.

Artist Credits - ©Vicki Sullivan

"There comes a time when the world gets quiet and the only thing left is your own heart. So you'd better learn the sound of it. Otherwise, you'll never understand what it's saying."

- Sarah Dessen
"Just Listen"

JUS' FEELING BLUE

It's dark now
I am very tired
just feeling blue
with thoughts of you
it's just time to rest now
it's just time to let you go

Cause you see that love of mine
she never really was anyhow
it was just all in my own mind anyway

So it's just time
with these thoughts of you
jus' feeling blue

It's that time
to just let that love go
jus' let you go

– Writer's Thoughts –

Just thinking about those past love things,
jus' feeling blue on this day.

Artist Credits © Skandi Dawani

" I dwell in possibility…"

— Emily Dickinson

POSSIBILITIES

We dwell in possibilities, you and me, living our dreams the way we do

Those possibilities I've chosen to believe in bringing with them a sense of curiosity, opening doors to our heart's desires to embrace them with the courage of who we are

It's the thought of possibility that transforms the promise of what our souls tell us we should be; for me, it's the promise that we have allowed our gentle souls to consummate with possibilities of our adore

Yes, what Emily said, " I dwell in possibility…" It's so true for you and me...

Living our world through our possibilities

– Writer's Thoughts –

I truly believe that only once in your life will you find
someone who can completely transform your life. You tell
them things that you've never shared with another, they
absorb everything you say and actually want to hear more.
You share hopes for the future, dreams that that never came
true, goals that were never achieved and the many
disappointments life has bestowed on you.
But in the end, it's the thought of those possibilities, for you
and me, living our dreams the way we do.

Artist Credits © Pita Nketiah

"Some birds are not meant to be caged, that's all. Their feathers are too bright, their songs too sweet and wild. So you let them go, or when you open the cage to feed them they somehow fly out past you. And the part of you that knows it was wrong to imprison them in the first place rejoices, but still, the place where you live is that much more drab and empty for their departure."

— Stephen King
Rita Hayworth and Shawshank Redemption

IT'S TIME

Took me a while to comprehend, just like before, I was fooling those desires of mine, I think it was just easier to wish it to be true, but it's time to accept the gravity of my anxiety, can't deny it anymore, it's just time

I knew it was a poor use of my precious time to chase those deliberations of mine; I just knew in the back of my mind, that it wasn't the right time

I knew I was agonizing with those regrets, those suspicions, and those grudges I harbored for way too long

Knowing all along that life was too short to be so bleak, I always knew it was time to turn the page and let it go

Cause you see, that love of mine, she never really was anyway; it was just all in my own mind anyhow

So it's just time to let it go

It's just that time

– Thoughts From a Younger Self –

It's dark now and I am very tired. I thought you were the one, it's just time now to rest. It was just all in my own mind anyhow, It's just that time to let those thoughts from a past love go. Just let her go.

Artist Credits - ©Erin Murphy

"It is not in the stars to hold our destiny but in ourselves."

— William Shakespeare

DESTINY

I was thinking it was our destiny, you and me —

As time kept changing, the seasons came to be, we just kept laying under the same dark sky, night after night, contemplating how it could be —

Never doubting those feelings, never letting that passion fade away, never altering that place in fate that was meant for you and me —

I'm thinkin' it's just our destiny to be —

– Writer's Thoughts –

Sometimes the dreams that come true are the dreams you never even knew you had.

Sometimes its just meant to be for you and me.

Artist Credits © Skandi Dawani

"Never fall in love?"
"Always," said the count. "I am always in love."

— Ernest Hemingway
" The Sun Also Rises "

OUT OF MY CONTROL

A vast concern was expunged from my soul cause I heard that love was out of my control

It doesn't matter anyhow ; cause it's going to happen anyway, you know that thing, that's out of my control

In time, my discretions will convey I'm all isolated, waiting for those desires; that's out of my control anyway

By the way, I'm sodden to the core and can't seem to loosen my grip on the realities of this thing we call love ; cause I heard anyway, it's out of my control anyhow

This concern that I had about this thing called love was expunged from my soul a long time ago

– Writer's Thoughts –

It has always been my notion that
there is never a time or place for true love. It just happens
unconsciously in a single unsuspecting moment. I heard,
anyway, it's out of my control anyhow.

Artist Credits - ©Erin Murphy
"Deidre"

"Until this moment, I had not realized that someone could break your heart twice along the very same fault lines."

— Jodi Picoult
My Sister's Keeper

FRACTURED

Deep inside, my heart is cracked
I can't help the way it behaves
This faded pulse within me
The one you gave to me
I can't help pursuing it
The desperation of not having it
Holding on to what once was
Keeping it locked away
Victimizing my soul
Slowly melting away —at what little I have left to give
With this fractured heart of mine

– Writer's Thoughts –

If you're searching for words that put your feeling of fractured heart into perspective – you won't find them.

You can learn every language and read every word ever written – but you'll never find the words to mend a broken heart; it's the admission fee for falling in love.

Artist Credits - ©Jenny Lou Crate Pena
All About the Stems

"There is a dark soul I hide as my possession: A riddled rose with Purple petals!"

— Afreen Rahat
Behind Her Eyes

WITHERED

I ought to have known she was the rose that tended to my garden, the one that was rooted deep within that soul of mine

I ought to have known by the way she cast her spell with such an ominous warmth to devour my spirit

I ought to have known that my fixations would lead to the pain that comes along with those thorns of cultivated desires; the more I hungered for that wild rose, the more I would bear the pricks of those tortuous thorns

I ought to have known those sorts of things when I tendered my heart to that feral flower rooted deep within the garden of my darkened soul

I ought to have known I was too young to comprehend how to nurture those crimson petals that shielded her core from all that hurt

If I would have jus' known before letting her decay into the lightless shadows as I watched her withered heart die from afar

I ought to have known; I was jus' too young to know

– Writer's Thoughts –

I always find solace in the crimson petals of a rose; it dares me to embrace my dark side, inspiring my poetic allure from memories of yesteryear.

JUS` THOUGHTS

"Night is purer than day; it is better for thinking, loving, and dreaming. At night everything is more intense, more true. The echo of words that have been spoken during the day takes on a new and deeper meaning."

— Elie Wiesel

Finale

Art Credits - © Just a Poet

" We write true things when we're not trying to write extraordinary things."

— Marty Rubin

HUMBLE GRANDIOSITY

Sometimes, I feel like an illuminator of grandeur, determined to make every littlest thing the very best it can be — not out of grandiosity but out of devotion to perfection, devotion paid for with my time and reflections, from those raw materials veering into delusional tales, per se...

Sometimes, I feel like a choreographer of thorny feelings across a multitude of resurrections — shaping the script that writes this poetry and countless others — poems that have long outlasted the importance that I felt when I composed them, poems that have helped me breathe life into my being

Sometimes, I sprinkle those words in such a way that mirrors my delusions of insignificance, feeling a profound responsibility to contribute my art through words with trifling and pathetic attempts at the illusion of grandeur — only to discover my own humility that shapes my soul and crafts my character into a humble grandiosity

– Writer's Thoughts –

Poets are hopeless romantics composing their words in solitude,
conveying our most winsome thoughts to another.

Poet's know that for those who love through their heartfelt
words, there is no such thing as emptiness in their souls.

Poet's can spend hours in silent pursuit to understand the
fragmented narrative of life, it is in this time of chaos I search for
a peaceful hope; for you see I'm jus' a Poet , I flourish in it.

Photography Credits © James (Pops) McManus

"The very basic core of a man's living spirit is his passion for adventure. The joy of life comes from our encounters with new experiences, and hence, there is no greater joy than to have an endlessly changing horizon, for each day to have a new and different sun."

Christopher McCandless

INTREPID

A man of youth, searching for a different awakened dawn, a spiritual pilgrimage, hiking with hitches of rides along the darkened skies of the day

A wanderer's spirit travels alone to become lost in the wilds of the White North of the Great, no longer burdened by the shackles of being pointless somewhere else

A soul traveling with a life of measured intrepidity and ponderance that the brave belong to all things

A man of youthful paragons of virtue on a spiritual pilgrimage, hiking with hitches of rides along the darkened skies of the day

Just tryin' to make it back to where he belongs, to the lands of cultivated farms afar

Just tryin' to be who he is meant to be, a bother to courageous warriors, a wanderer of gallant intrepidation, no longer burdened by the shackles of being pointless somewhere else

– Writer's Thoughts –

This piece was inspired by reflections of a father's tale of a man's youth. As a boy, I would listen for hours as my Pops recounted stories of his travels as a young man. To this day, those memories of his gallant adventures are still measured in my soul by his resolute fearlessness, fortitude, and endurance as an intrepid explorer.

Artist Credits - ©Jenny Lou Crate Pena
Twilight Stroll

"A melancholy-looking man, he had the appearance of one who has searched for the leak in life's gas pipe with a lighted candle."

— P.G. Wodehouse

COLORS OF INCURIOSITY

Those moody colors give rise to incuriosity, threatening negativity, bringing with it those gray hues always at a time of complication

Never an announcement, just showing up like those uninvited family members with troubled intentions

Painting those opaque dyed metaphors mimicking the mood of my emotions

Just like those blues defining my perpetual funk, or those reds illustrating an ignorant rage of bitterness, perhaps my least invited, that color of dim gray shepherding my anxieties

But the ones that irritate me the most are my favorite colors, purple and lilac. That purple hyacinth is so symbolic of my darkness

Those damn spectrum of colors of incuriosity associated with my negativity mimics the mood of my emotions

- Writer's Thoughts -

I struggle with darkness from time to time; as a writer, I find myself drawn to poetry to find solace, comfort, and solidarity and understand better my experiences—as well as the experiences of those who deal with depression in ways that don't mirror mine at all.

Depression is often felt to be colorblind; however, for me, I constantly see my darkness through a spectrum of colors of coldness associated with the melancholy of negativity. Giving rise to those moody colors of incuriosity.

Artist Credits - ©Jenny Lou Crate Pena
Morning Tea

"The window is where curiosities meet. Insiders are curious about the outside, and outsiders are curious about the inside! When the window is opened, those who wonder flow towards the place they wonder, those inside are out, those outside are in!"

— Mehmet Murat ildan

WINDOWS INTO A SOUL

I've always felt at peace in the hour just before dawn, when the darkness seems to give way slowly to a mist, at that early hour, I can sit alone by an open window for hours listening only to those birds of song with the rustling of thoughts into my introspections

A gentle breeze filling my ambitions with a soft tenderness, pursuing what that window symbolizes - a place to discover the world from a new lens of opportunities, beginnings, and intuitions

A place without hesitation or self-doubt, an openness that confers with my vision, a place where everything is written from new insights

Sometimes I can't help but wonder if I'm indeed looking out through that open window or literally looking in towards my own thoughts of introspection as I see the world in that new light

– Writer's Thoughts –

A writer should be able to open a window or two for others to see
the world and themselves in a new light.
Anything less is just intellectual self–indulgence.

Artist Credits - ©Jenny Lou Crate Pena

"The artist's painting reminds me of Andrew Wyeth's "November First". With it's tattered stalks in a harvested field, capturing the cold damp of late autumn, portraying the inevitable cycles of decay and renewal.
Stirring our imaginations like no other, reminding us to slow and to be thankful."

— a Poet Afar

NOVEMBER'S MIRTH

How beautiful it was, that smell of death, those scents that only decaying leaves can yield, those musky odors that rise from the darkened earth as lifeless waste, with damp aromas of wet soil with brown and yellow leaves absorbing into my senses gently as the season stirred into a late Autumn chill

Listening to those lingering birds serenading delicate songs from withering trees, embracing November's arriving mirth, ushering in with it tantalizing fragrances filling my nose with smells of curling chimney smoke, decaying matter, and things baking in ovens

Aah, November stirring our imaginations like no other, reminding us to slow and to be thankful

– Writer's Thoughts –

November it's a season all to itself. The calming reminder that death happens, pausing is a good thing, and the time of renewal is already in place.

Artist Credits © Kinga E. Vnuk
" O Come O Come Emmanuel "
Oil on Canvas

"Silent night, holy night. All is calm, all is bright. Round yon Virgin Mother and Child. Holy Infant so tender and mild. Sleep in heavenly peace. Sleep in heavenly peace."

— Joseph Mohr

A SILENT NIGHT

On this silent of nights, a darkness has occupied my spirit; it's the same place that once was reserved for those splendors of peace

In this holiest of nights, my soul is but a shadowed hole that has obscured into a mute sadness, withdrawing into the depths of a lusterless core

On this night, when all is to be calm, bright, so tender and mild with a heavenly peace; I should be full of blissful joy, but on this night, a soul has been laced yet again with misguided intentions of my complicit vulnerabilities

On this night, a stillness has coerced me back to the corners of a darkened soul

A place I know all too well, a place thought to be latched forever
A place that has been reborn with darkness on this holiest of silent nights

– Writer's Thoughts –

In the season of silent nights, as I gaze into those distant stars. I am consumed with a strange sense of darkness, inviting me to write these words that are plaguing my thoughts these days.

Artist Credits ©Darya Karabchuk

"This winter, there will be no voices, no glimpses, no arms, only the fabric of poetry to keep me warm."

— Sanober Khan

A WINTER DARK

With the Yuletide season fading to a dulling commemorative, an emptiness unhurriedly creeps in, bringing with it that dead feeling of loneliness

With those dark intervals between long days, it seems to me that poetry will be an obsession, that words of stanzas will conflict with the approaching darkness, filling that despairing void inside; we can ignore it, avoid all thoughts of it, for only so long, becoming voluble to no end

Sensing that winter's nothingness, when my soul is silent if it speaks at all, it speaks through poetry

Only needing a touch of provocation to breathe life into those words, conveying wisdom to understand that this dark winter silence is but a warm, inspiring companion, a time to let those poetic introspections breathe

– Writer's Thoughts –

For me, the passing of the Yuletide season always brings a sense of melancholy, a feeling of lonely emptiness. During those times of darkness, I chose to fill that void with my delusional mutterings of poetry, simply letting those poetic introspections breathe.

Artist Credits ©Darya Karabchuk

"I am not what I ought to be, I am not what I want to be, I am not what I hope to be in another world; but still, I am not what I once used to be, and by the grace of God I am what I am"

— John Newton

LES RÉVÉLATION
` DISCLOSING OF TRUTH `

All my life I have felt a sense of obligation that at times has been debilitating, now an older self comprehends with age comes reflective perspicuity

This wisdom of enlightenment brightens those dark hollows of my misguided realities, bringing forth a moment of revelation

What if suddenly we just became mindful of the idea that our lives as we lived them were just a misinterpretation of who we really were meant to be

What if we were only conforming to serve, to achieve, to succeed, to impress, to be esteemed by those whose only purposes were to deplete our goodwilled intentions

What if as we performed on life's proverbial stage we were just the supporting cast to the bedlam controlling our expressive orientations

What if we simply knew all along who we wanted to be, and not that semblance that we were told to be

What if all along we were just who we ought to be, just being who we turned out to just be

– Writer's Thoughts –

Life has away of transforming our perspective on just who we really are, disclosing our truths. Sometimes the circumstances we live in shapes who we might try to be. I have discovered through age comes wisdom to break free from the delusional chains that life can shackle us with. With time and maturity we eventually accept and just become who we really ought to be.

Artist Credits © Khurram Amir

“ Without description, without imagery, no poem can function, without luster that poetry will be even more leaden, bogged down by the pale, shapeless weight of its artistic source, like a log overtaken by ghostly fungi sinking into a bog, just colorless and devoid of an illuminated spirit, just tarnished words on a piece of paper. “

— a Poet from Afar

TARNISHED WORDS

Lately, my words have been feeling a bit unpolished, like that old wooden box of vintage cutlery that's hardly ever used

Those words that once flowed from my pen so easily are starting to have no luster or shame; they're just telling me to come back later; that ink is beginning to dry up, just like those thoughts that once meandered through my premonitions

Toiling with my inspirations as if they were some sort of sarcastic affliction, notifying me of the demise of those syllables I so desperately chase to count

That poetic ink that once flowed from my pen for yearning minds to comprehend is now just dulling tarnished words on a page of textile devoid of poetic coherence

– Writer's Thoughts –-

I always feel that my poetry must be scaled with descriptions derived from its source, such in a way that you can hear the words slithering through the grass, vines, and leaves of the page on which it's written. It must be variegated, and if its inspiration operates in colorless realms, it must emit the grey mists and bright blankness of the depths of that those words were begotten, feeling as if each word written must glisten with poetic imagery.

Artist Credits ©Darya Karabchuk

"The role of a writer is not to say what we all can say, but what we are unable to say."

—Anaïs Nin

THROUGH THE VOID

At the end of my suffering there was an entry into a dark peaceful void, it was a feeling of ease that couldn't be explained, a serenity that was so vividly recalled

In the opaque dim hue cast throughout the night air, I could hear rumors of shallow condolences whispering throughout the darkness

Then there was nothing at all, just a fragile moon that flickered over my soul as it was gently laid to rest in the dark rich fertile soil

It was then that I realized the heavy weight, of a burdened soul had been lifted, it was then all the things I feared were unable to haunt that sanity of mine anymore, it was then as the warm earth caressed my tired spirit that there was a final peace that spoke in a language of serene tranquility

It was only then, in that dark void, I knew my suffering had dearly departed with those shallow condolences

– Writer's Thoughts –

As my existence lures nearer to finality, there is a feeling of relief that can not be described with mere words alone.
Coming with it is a serenity that there will finally be a peace that will rest with my burdened soul, a harmony that speaks in a language of peaceful tranquility.
Only then will I know the true feeling of ascension from those burdens I've carried for too long.

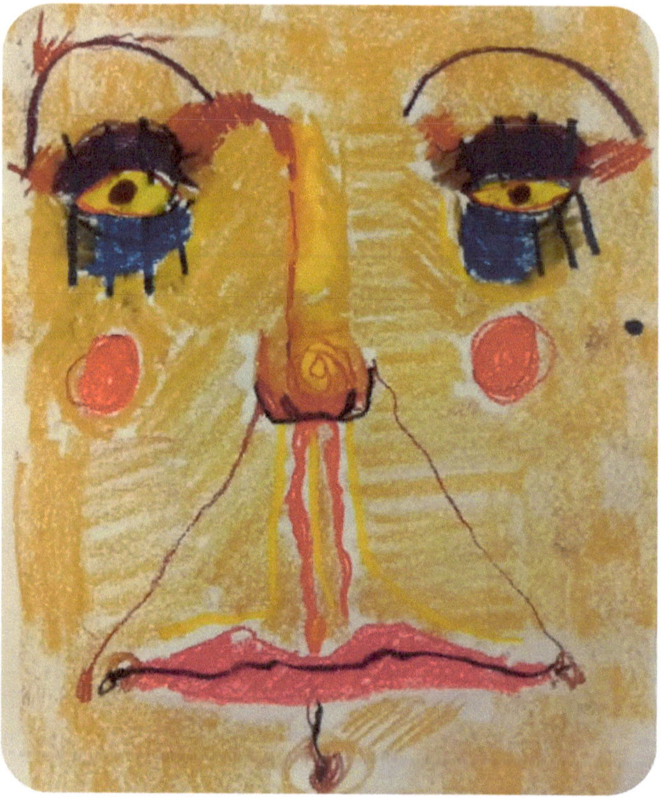

Artist Credits © Emma Eevantytär

"Despite my pain, I felt not the regret of an ending, but the foreboding of a beginning."

—Robin Hobb
"Fool's Errand"